THE
ANCIENT
GREEKS

*W*ith special thanks to Megan Cifarelli,
Norbert Schimmel Fellow in the Art of the Mediterranean
at the Metropolitan Museum of Art, New York City,
for her invaluable assistance in
reading the manuscript

THE
ANCIENT
GREEKS

VIRGINIA SCHOMP

BENCHMARK BOOKS

MARSHALL CAVENDISH
NEW YORK

Benchmark Books

Marshall Cavendish Corporation
99 White Plains Road
Tarrytown, New York 10591-9001

Library of Congress Cataloging-in-Publication Data
Schomp, Virginia, date.
   The ancient Greeks / by Virginia Schomp.
      p.   cm. — (Cultures of the past)
   Includes bibliographical references and index.
   ISBN 0-7614-0070-2
   1. Greece—History—Juvenile literature. [1. Greece—History.] I. Title. II. Series.
   DF77.S365   1996
   938—dc20   95-7101

SUMMARY: Traces the rise and fall of Greek civilization from the Bronze Age to the Roman conquest, discussing the history, culture, mythology, and legacy of the Ancient Greeks.

Printed and bound in Italy

Book design by Carol Matsuyama
Photo research by Debbie Needleman

Front cover: The so-called Mask of Agamemnon, one of the golden death masks buried with the kings of Mycenaean Greece
Back cover: A flute player and dancer perform through the ages. Painting on an ancient Greek drinking cup, c. 520 B.C.E.

Photo Credits
Front cover: courtesy of Nimatallah/Art Resource, NY; back cover: courtesy of the British Museum, London/Bridgeman Art Library, London; pages 6, 9, 13, 19, 21, 37, 40, 64, 65: Robert Frerck/Odyssey Productions/Hillstrom Stock Photo; pages 7, 16, 17, 23, 27, 35, 57, 67, 71: The Granger Collection, New York; pages 8, 10: National Archaeological Museum, Athens/Bridgeman Art Library, London; page 24: Bibliothéque Nationale, Paris/Bridgeman Art Library, London; page 29 *(bottom)*: Louvre, Paris/Giraudon/Bridgeman Art Library, London; page 12: Vanni/Art Resource, NY; pages 14, 52, 55: The Bettmann Archive; page 22: Nimatallah/Art Resource, NY; pages 28, 45, 60, 66: Scala/Art Resource, NY; pages 26, 29 *(top)*, 33, 43, 49: Erich Lessing/Art Resource, NY; page 31: Envision/Jean Higgins; page 38: Werner Forman/Art Resource, NY; page 46: Bury Art Gallery & Museum/Bridgeman Art Library, London; page 47: Olympia Museum, Athens/Bridgeman Art Library, London; page 51: Prado, Madrid/Index/Bridgeman Art Library, London; page 58: British Museum, London/Bridgeman Art Library, London; page 62: Roy Miles Gallery, London/Bridgeman Art Library, London; page 68: Envision/Henryk T. Kaiser; page 69: Dave Bartruff; page 70: Jeffrey Aaronson/Network Aspen

CONTENTS

CHAPTER ONE

DAYS OF DARKNESS, DAYS OF DAWN

Not long ago, most scholars traced Greek history back to 776 B.C.E.* That was the year of the Greeks' first dated record, a list of the winners at the Olympic Games. Greek poets had written of earlier centuries, of glorious battles and ancient kingdoms rich in gold. But to historians, these were just fairy tales. Then a startling discovery knocked the experts on their ears.

In 1871 German archaeologist Heinrich Schliemann (HINE-reehk SHLEE-mahn) unearthed the "mythical" city of Troy. Thousands of adventurers armed with picks and shovels scrambled to follow Schliemann's lead. Soon their discoveries of buried citadels, colossal palaces, and royal graveyards overflowing with

*Many systems of dating have been used by different cultures throughout history. This series of books uses B.C.E. (Before Common Era) and C.E. (Common Era) instead of B.C. (Before Christ) and A.D. (Anno Domini) out of respect for the diversity of the world's peoples.

Massive stone horns top the palace at Knossos, center of the brilliant Minoan civilization. These horns honored the bull, a sacred animal in the Minoan religion.

HEINRICH SCHLIEMANN: SEEKER OF LOST WORLDS

When Heinrich Schliemann was eight years old, he made a solemn vow to devote his life to finding the lost city of Troy. Bedtime stories of ancient Greek heroes who battled one-eyed monsters and outsmarted crafty villains had always fascinated Heinrich. He especially liked the story of the Trojan War, the heroic battle waged by Greece over the beautiful Helen of Troy. But unlike most people, Heinrich believed that the ancient stories were true. In 1868 he left Germany for Greece to prove it.

Using thousand-year-old poetry as his guide, Schliemann journeyed from Greece east to neighboring Turkey. There he found not one but *nine* Troys, one on top of the other. Troy VII was the level he was seeking—the ancient city besieged for ten years by a heroic Greek army.

But what of the Greeks who conquered Troy—Achilles, Ajax, King Agamemnon? Schliemann went in search of these heroes beneath the thick walls surrounding the ruined Greek city Mycenae. The royal graves he uncovered over-flowed with gold and jewels. As he lifted the golden death mask from the face of a corpse, he believed he looked upon Agamemnon. He was wrong. The burial chamber belonged not to the famous twelfth-century B.C.E. king but to an unknown ruler of the late seventeenth century B.C.E., the age of the early Mycenaean civilization.

Many people criticized Heinrich Schliemann. They argued that his enthusiasm sometimes led him to do careless work and make wild claims. But that same enthusiasm, combined with hard work and faith, brought to light a great civilization that had lain for centuries in darkness.

treasure proved that many of the people and places from the ancient legends really had existed. Centuries before the supposed beginning of Greek history, wondrous and undreamed-of civilizations had flourished by the Aegean Sea.

Birth of the Greeks

Four thousand years ago, tall, graceful sailing ships dotted the blue Aegean. Their home port was Crete, an island fifty miles south of mainland Greece and the site of the region's first great civilization.

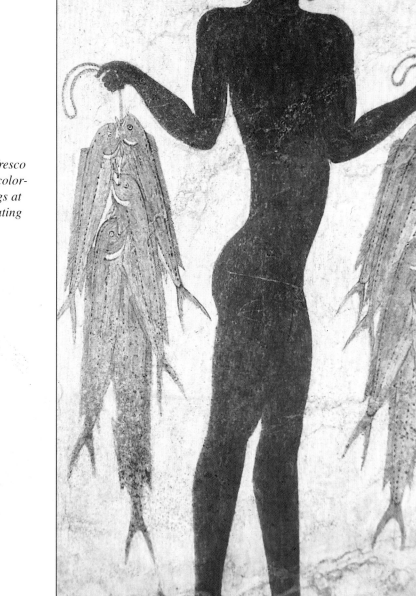

The fisherman fresco is one of many colorful wall paintings at Knossos celebrating everyday life in ancient Crete.

Named Minoan after legendary King Minos of Crete, this brilliant civilization reached its height between 1700 and 450 B.C.E. The slender, dark-haired Minoans grew wealthy through trade across the surrounding waters. They built fairy-tale palaces with brightly colored wall paintings and delicate ornaments of gold and precious jewels. Their paintings show a joyful people who loved games and sport and delighted in nature's beauties.

While the Minoans flourished on Crete, another civilization grew strong on the Greek mainland. The mainlanders were a war-like people who lived in huge fortress-cities, each ruled by an all-powerful king. The kings built splendid palaces surrounded by walls so massive that it took two mules to pull just one of the smallest stones. The richest and strongest of their settlements sat on a high hill in Mycenae (my-SEE-nee), the city that gave its name to their entire civilization.

For many years the Mycenaeans (my-se-NEE-uhns) of mainland Greece and the Minoans of Crete lived side by side in

Lion Gate, the main entrance to the palace at Mycenae

9

peace. The Mycenaeans were impressed by Minoan culture. Their kings hired artists and craftsmen from Crete to work on the mainland, sharing their knowledge. Over time the Mycenaeans adopted much of Crete's customs, religion, and art.

Then, around 1400 B.C.E., the Mycenaeans invaded their island neighbor. Soon Mycenaean warlords sat on Cretan thrones, and the Minoans faded into history. The Mycenaean civilization grew to its height of power, with trade and influence stretching as far as Spain, Italy, Syria, and the banks of Egypt's Nile. But even

The graves of Mycenae's royal families held many treasures, including elaborate weapons like this bronze dagger. The lion-hunt scene is crafted in gold and silver.

massive stone walls could not keep out foreign invaders lured by rumors of treasure. Around 1200 B.C.E. Mycenaean citadels fell one by one to waves of fierce tribesmen, who some historians think came from northwest Greece. Within one hundred years all the major Mycenaean cities had been abandoned or destroyed.

The Dark Age

Like leaves caught in a strong wind, the Mycenaeans scattered before their invaders. Many were killed or enslaved. Many banded together in small tribal groups and settled in poor farming villages. And many Mycenaeans escaped to peace and freedom by journeying east across the Aegean Sea.

No written records survive from this period of upheaval that historians call the Dark Age. But around 800 B.C.E. a much-changed Greece emerged into the light of history. The well-organized city-kingdoms of Mycenaean Greece were gone. In their place was a new Greece, a scattered nation made of small communities on the mainland, island colonies in the Aegean, and colonies along the western coast of Asia Minor. Each colony had its own name—Samos, Miletus, Ephesus—but together they were known as Ionia.

Trade was brisk between the mainland cities and the Ionian colonies. The constant exchange of pottery, cloth, metalwork, and other goods, along with a shared language and religion, bound together the far-flung settlements. The long Dark Age had ended, and the foundations were laid for the most glorious period of Greek history.

Rise of the City-States

Many of the new Greek settlements had been built around the shelter of a high hilltop, or acropolis. Gradually all the villages surrounding each acropolis joined together to form a united city-state, or polis (PAH-lehs). In the eighth century B.C.E. hundreds of independent poleis (PAH-lays) formed throughout Greece.

Each city-state had its own patron deity—a god who watched over the polis from the temple built on its acropolis. The people took pride in their special god and in the traditions and way of life of their polis. Their patriotism, along with the need to provide for a growing population, led to a vast colonizing movement. Beginning in the eighth century B.C.E., the city-states began sending out adventurers to claim new lands. By the sixth century B.C.E. hundreds of Greek trading colonies had been established in what is today Spain, Italy, Sicily, Egypt, Libya, Africa, the Ukraine—throughout the whole of the Mediterranean and Black Sea regions.

During this time of new beginnings, great changes also came to the mother cities. The early poleis were governed by nobles—the heads of powerful families—who often used their position to increase their wealth. Over time the power of the nobles lessened, and a new concern for the rights of ordinary people blossomed. Gradually the idea that the city-state should serve the will of *all* citizens took root. Polis came to mean not just a place but its people, too, with all citizens directly involved in their government. From that point on, the history of Greece is the history of its city-states. Proud and independent, each polis developed its own rich art, customs, institutions, and gods.

The Acropolis of Athens, with its many temples, theaters, and other important buildings. The Parthenon, temple of the city's patron deity, Athena, rises on the right.

The Golden Age

The two most powerful city-states of ancient Greece—Athens and Sparta—developed just miles apart by land but worlds apart in the lives and character of their people.

A port city on the Aegean, at the crossroads of overseas trade, Athens opened its arms to the customs and culture of many lands. The Athenians welcomed new ideas. They encouraged public debate and even disagreement with the state. They created the world's first democracy—the first government ruled by the governed. In the fifth and fourth centuries B.C.E., Athens served as a model of excellence for the rest of the Greek world. During this Golden Age, the work of Athens's writers, artists, architects, scientists, statesmen, and philosophers achieved an originality and beauty that the world has rarely seen.

One hundred fifty miles from Athens and far from the sea, a remarkably different culture also reached its height during the Golden Age. The people of Sparta disapproved

PERICLES: MAN OF VISION

The father of Greek democracy had an unusually long, pointed face that earned him the nickname "Onion Head." Critics also called Pericles (PEHR-ih-kleez) cold, stubborn, and conceited. But to his admirers these were just the qualities of a great leader whose brilliance and clear sense of mission set him apart from ordinary men.

Pericles' mission was to make Athens a "school for Greece." In this model city, people would live like gods, devoting their lives to the creative spirit and the search for truth. A quiet, serious man, Pericles spoke seldom, and softly. But when he spoke, the Athenians listened. For over thirty years, from 461 to 429 B.C.E., they elected and reelected him as their leader.

Under Pericles Athens built a strong navy and a mighty empire. It created a democracy in which all free male citizens, rich and poor, had the right to vote and to take turns serving in important government posts. Pericles supported and encouraged the work of Athenian writers, artists, architects, scientists, and philosophers. In the atmosphere of individual excellence that Pericles nourished, Athens's Golden Age thrived.

of trade, of contact with outsiders, of new inventions and ideas. Sparta was one of the few city-states that never developed a democracy. Throughout its history it was ruled by kings and nobles, and disagreement with its rulers was punished by death.

Spartan society was built around military discipline. From the day he turned seven, every male citizen was expected to dedicate his life to learning the skills of war. The Spartans built no glorious temples and produced no lasting works of art or literature. But a lifetime of physical training and strict discipline made their army the strongest and bravest in all the world.

All infants born in Sparta were brought before public officials for examination. Only those who looked likely to grow into strong, healthy citizens were allowed to live; sickly infants were taken to the mountains and abandoned.

The Greco-Persian Wars

Greece needed all its armies in the fifth century B.C.E., when King Darius I of Persia turned his warships toward the Greek mainland. The vast Persian empire stretched across much of Asia and the

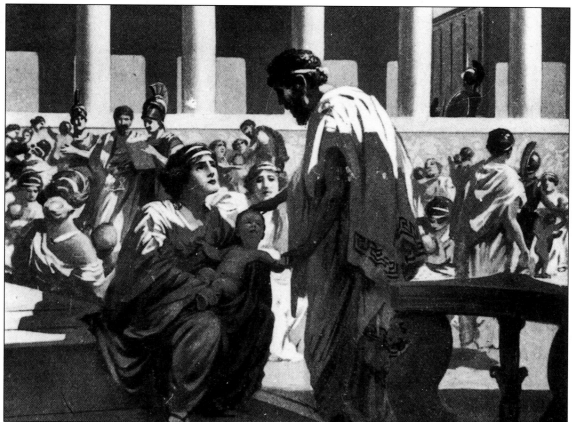

14

Middle East. Now Darius planned to add Greece to his domain.

The Persians' first target was Athens. But in a desperate battle in 490 B.C.E., a force of nine thousand Athenian foot soldiers charged and defeated sixty thousand Persian invaders. Ten years later Darius's son Xerxes (ZERK-zeez) returned with a Persian army now two hundred thousand strong. This time the invaders were soundly defeated by a united army drawn from all the poleis. Athens and Sparta led the Greek forces, and in their stunning victory the two cities reached new heights of power and fame.

Greek Against Greek

The unity of the city-states that drove back the Persians was short-lived. Two poleis as different as Athens and Sparta could not remain allies for long. In the decades following the Greco-Persian Wars, Athens rose to its greatest glory. The Athenians produced their finest works of art and literature, built their most magnificent monuments, spread democracy to other poleis, and expanded their empire abroad. Meanwhile, Sparta watched in jealousy and suspicion.

At last Sparta declared war on Athens, and all the city-states were forced to take sides. Many Greek cities, afraid the Athenian empire was becoming too powerful and too arrogant in its power, sided with the Spartans. The Peloponnesian (peh-luh-puh-NEE-zhehn) War—named for Peloponnesus, the peninsula south of the mainland that was home to Sparta and many of its allies—lasted twenty-seven years. Each side enjoyed great victories; each suffered terrible losses.

In 413 B.C.E., in a battle off the coast of Sicily, south of Italy, Sparta destroyed the entire Athenian fleet. Athens was deserted by many of its allies. Its wealth was spent, its food supplies nearly gone, its people starving and exhausted. As the fourth century drew to a bitter close, Athens surrendered to Sparta.

Macedonian Conquest

Victory in the Peloponnesian War gave Sparta dominance over all the city-states. But the stern Spartans had no idea how to govern

A nineteenth-century artist's view of Sparta. Young boys train for a life of harsh discipline and military service.

people who were used to freedom and democracy. For thirty years a series of land and sea battles pitted polis against polis, Greek against Greek. These small wars further weakened and divided the weary city-states.

While the Greeks squabbled, a new danger grew unnoticed on their doorstep. A bold and skillful general, Philip II, seized the throne of Macedonia, a region in the far north of mainland Greece. Philip united the warlike tribes of Macedonia and built them into a well-trained army. In 338 B.C.E. that army challenged a patched-together force of foot soldiers from the city-states Athens and Thebes. The Macedonians wiped out the opposition. All across Greece men lay down their swords.

In his victory Philip accomplished what no Greek leader ever had—lasting unity among the city-states. He offered to withdraw his soldiers and allow the Greeks to govern themselves. In exchange he demanded that the independent poleis join together in a united federation, accepting him as their commander in a campaign to conquer Persia.

King Philip II was murdered by one of his own officers before he could realize his dreams of empire. But the son who took his place would carry those dreams further than Philip had ever imagined.

Alexander and the Hellenistic Age

In 335 B.C.E. Philip's son Alexander set out to conquer the world. Within three years he had captured the entire eastern Persian empire without losing a single battle. His united Greek forces went on to conquer Egypt, western Persia, western India, and

Alexander the Great battles the Persians. This sixteenth-century Persian miniature painting shows Alexander toward the left, riding a tall gray horse.

present-day Afghanistan and Pakistan. Alexander the Great's conquests stretched over one million square miles—the largest empire the world had ever known.

Wherever he claimed victory, Alexander founded cities modeled on the Greek poleis. The first and most famous of these cities, Alexandria, Egypt, became the world's most important center of trade and learning.

In 324 B.C.E., after ten years of fighting, the worn-out Greek army refused to go on. Reluctantly Alexander turned for home. The journey would be his last. Alexander the Great died in a soldier's tent from fever and exhaustion at the age of thirty-two. For the next forty years his generals battled for possession of his vast empire. In the end Alexander's realm was divided into three: the Ptolemaic (tah-leh-MAY-ihk) kingdom in Egypt, the Seleucid (seh-LOO-sehd) kingdom in Asia, and the Macedonian kingdom in Macedonia and Greece.

ALEXANDER THE GREAT: EMPIRE BUILDER

At sixteen he led an army that put down a revolt and founded a city. By the age of twenty-two he had carved out an empire that stretched from Greece to Egypt to India.

He was uncommonly handsome. He was recklessly brave. He was loyal to his friends, kind to his soldiers, honorable in his agreements, and so renowned for his mercy that many cities simply opened their gates to the conqueror. Yet he was also known for fits of rage and acts of cruelty so ferocious that some historians call him half insane.

Alexander the Great spent his youth studying under the famous Greek philosopher Aristotle. He grew up believing that the Greeks were superior to all other peoples. He also believed that he was a descendant of the legendary Greek warrior Achilles. Clearly, Alexander reasoned, he had been chosen by the gods to lead Greece to its rightful place as ruler of one united world.

"It is a lovely thing to live with courage, and to die, leaving behind an everlasting renown," said Alexander the Great. This brilliant soldier, this man of ambition and contradictions, certainly left behind a lasting fame. But he left far more than that. Through Alexander's conquests, Greek civilization touched and transformed the world.

The marble sarcophagus, or coffin, of Alexander the Great is carved with scenes from the life of a fierce and fearless conqueror.

In the three centuries following Alexander's death, the power of the Greek poleis slowly faded. But during this Hellenistic Age (for Hellene, the Greeks' name for their homeland), Greek culture took root all across the known world. In the cities that Alexander had founded and Greek settlers had filled, the Greek language dominated government and trade. Greek architecture, art, and laws were copied. Greek philosophy and science advanced. Even in its old age, the ancient Greek civilization flowered.

Roman Rule

As the Greek poleis declined, a mighty kingdom rose to their west, in Rome. In 86 B.C.E. the Romans occupied Athens. Soon they were masters of the entire Greek mainland. Greece and Macedonia were combined into a single province, ruled by a Roman governor. The Romans then marched east to seize, one by one, the lands Alexander had claimed. In fifty short years the

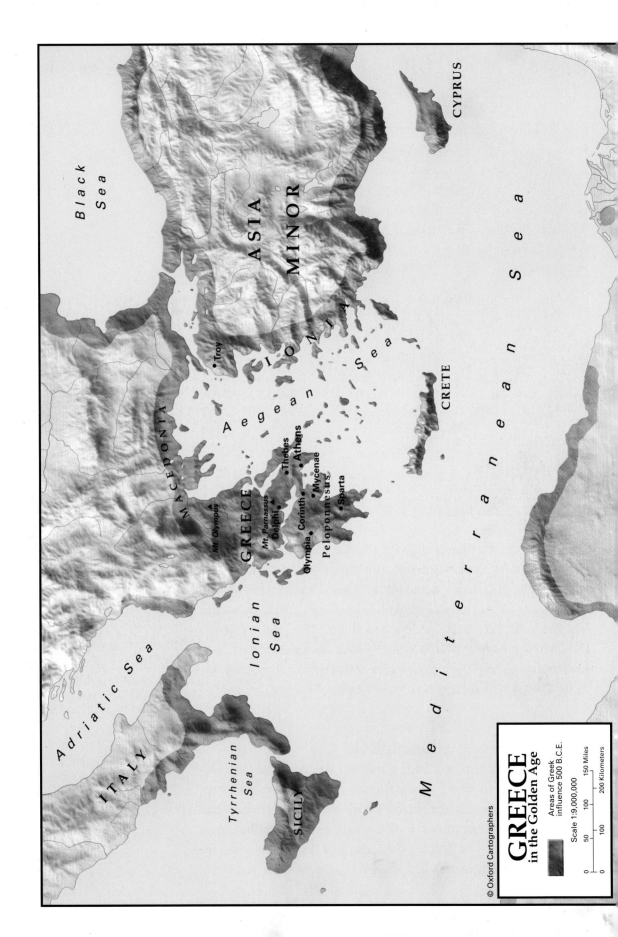

CYPRUS

Black Sea

ASIA

MINOR

I O N I A

•Troy

A e g e a n   S e a

A   d   r   i   a   t   i   c   S   e   a

MACEDONIA

GREECE

▲ Mt. Olympus

Mt. Parnassus
Delphi ▲
•Thebes
•Athens
Olympia• •Corinth •Mycenae
Peloponnesus •Sparta

CRETE

M   e   d   i   t   e   r   r   a   n   e   a   n   S   e   a

I   o   n   i   a   n   S   e   a

ITALY

T   y   r   r   h   e   n   i   a   n   S   e   a

SICILY

© Oxford Cartographers

GREECE
in the Golden Age

Areas of Greek
influence 500 B.C.E.

Scale 1:9,000,000

0   50   100   150 Miles

0   100   200 Kilometers

Roman Empire reigned supreme over the entire Mediterranean region and much of Europe, the Middle East, and northern Africa.

The Romans admired and imitated Greek art and customs. They spread Greek culture throughout their vast empire, preserving its heritage for future generations. Though its power might fade and its monuments crumble, ancient Greece was never truly conquered, for the light of its genius continues to instruct and inspire us today.

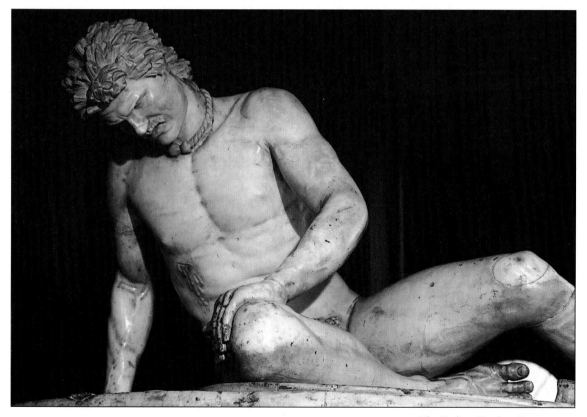

The Dying Gaul, *a Roman copy of a Greek statue. Roman copies helped preserve Greek art and spread Greek culture across the world.*

CHAPTER TWO

CULTURAL TRIUMPHS

The history of a people is more than a record of its battles and its kings. To begin to know the ancient Greeks, we must look deeper, into the creative forces that filled their lives with fire and beauty.

Literature: The Ageless Song

From the poets and scholars of ancient Greece came works of uncommon beauty that gave the world brand-new ways of expressing age-old concerns.

Epic Poetry

The Mycenaean Greeks left no written literature. Baked clay tablets still hold lists of the goods in their storerooms and offerings to their gods. But stories of the Mycenaeans' past and their heroes were not written; they were sung.

Wandering minstrels—poet-musicians who played a stringed instrument called the lyre—entertained Mycenaean nobles with long songs about the heroic deeds of their ancestors. During the Dark Age, these oral histories traveled with Greek colonists to the new Ionian settlements across the Aegean. Then, in the eighth century B.C.E., the old stories found a new and glorious voice. For the first time the traditional tales of Mycenaean heroes were written down, in imaginative histories called epic poems.

The first and most famous of the Greek epic poets was Homer. His two long poems, the

Apollo, the Greek god of poets and musicians, wears a crown of myrtle leaves and plays a minstrel's lyre.

The poet Homer calls for inspiration from a Muse—one of the Greek goddesses of art, literature, music, and science.

Iliad (IH-lee-uhd) and the *Odyssey* (AH-duh-see), tell the story of the Trojan War. In the *Iliad*, King Agamemnon of Mycenae and a company of mighty Greek heroes wage war against the walled city of Troy over the kidnapping of the beautiful Greek queen Helen. The long battle ends with a famous trick—the Mycenaeans gain entrance to Troy by hiding inside a huge wooden horse. The *Odyssey* recounts the magical adventures of the Greek hero Odysseus (oh-DIH-see-uhs) on his journey home from the war.

Homer's epics were treasured by the ancient Greeks as both history and bible. The *Iliad* and the *Odyssey* restored the nearly forgotten heroes of the Greeks' earlier days. Their organized presentation of the Greek gods made them the foundation of the Greek religion. In centuries to come, the works of Greece's first great poet would continue to inspire writers all across the Western world.

Down through the ages, many artists have created images of the famous Trojan horse. This is a fifteenth-century painting by French artist Raoul Lefevre.

The Greek Theater

Two hundred years after Homer, the Greeks gave the world a new form of expression—drama, or the play. The earliest Greek plays were religious ceremonies in which a chorus sang and acted out stories about the gods. Later plays told the legends of Greek heroes, too, and included actors who separated from the chorus and spoke their own lines.

Drama reached its height in the Golden Age, when huge open-air theaters were built all across Greece. Dramatic programs often lasted an entire day, with performances of both tragedies and comedies. Aeschylus (EHS-kuh-luhs), Sophocles (SAH-fuh-kleez), and Euripides (yuh-RIH-puh-deez) were the most famous Greek playwrights of tragedy. Their dramas dealt with human pride and punishment, the anger of the gods, and people's struggles against unchangeable fate. Aristophanes (ehr-uh-STAH-fuh-neez), the master of Greek comedy, wrote plays that poked fun at human weaknesses like vanity and laziness.

Greek actors were always men. They played both the male and female roles. Greek playgoers made an enthusiastic, sometimes difficult audience. Perched on hard stone benches, they sat out a whole day's program, snacking on nuts, drinking wine, applauding, hissing, and occasionally tossing olive pits. Even viewers in the back rows had good seats—the actors wore oversized masks that projected their voices and made them easy to tell apart. The chorus sang and danced. "Gods" descended on wooden platforms. Painted backgrounds turned for an instant change of scene. All in all it was a spectacular performance combining music, dance, acting, poetry, and art.

Writing History

The Greeks were the Western world's first writers of prose history—the first to use everyday language to look beyond the gods for the natural causes of events.

In the fifth century B.C.E. the "father of history," Herodotus (hih-RAH-duh-tuhs), explored the Mediterranean region. Herodotus wrote long accounts of the wars, geography, customs, and legends he encountered in his travels. His writings are not always accurate. He passes on fables about headless men with eyes in

The Theatre of Delphi, built in 160 B.C.E. on the slope of Mount Parnassus. The theater held five thousand spectators in thirty-five rows of seats.

their chests and giant bats guarding Asian lakes where spices grow. But in his accounts we also find volumes of fascinating, factual information about the peoples of the ancient world.

Fifty years after Herodotus, the historian Thucydides (thoo-SIH-duh-deez) wrote about life in Greece from the end of the Greco-Persian Wars through Sparta's conquest of Athens. Thucydides wrote only what he knew to be true. His accounts are less entertaining than Herodotus's, but more reliable.

Thucydides' histories are detailed records of people's actions; from Herodotus we learn about their customs and characters. Between them the two men invented the styles that Western writers of history have used ever since.

Herodotus, "father of history," reads his works before an attentive audience of Greeks.

Art and Architecture: The Dream of Beauty

Time has destroyed most of the masterpieces of ancient Greek art. The few left to us are faded, broken, crumbled. But through the damage we still can trace a glorious past.

Pottery and Painting

The Minoans of ancient Crete excelled at the potter's wheel. Their delicate vases, cups, and jars were glazed in every shade imaginable, from crimson red to turquoise blue. The Minoans' skill passed to the Mycenaeans and then was lost in the Dark Age. The Greeks who emerged from that long period of upheaval had to invent the art of pottery-making all over again.

Gradually fine artistry returned to the potter's craft. Between 800 B.C.E. and the Macedonian conquest, the Greek city-states—especially Athens—produced the most valued pottery of the ancient Western world. Their vessels were both strong and graceful. Adorning them were human figures etched in clay and brought to life with gleaming glaze. Gods warred, heroes battled, ordinary people worked and played. On the faces of these figures delight, pain, and longing speak as vividly today as on the centuries-old day of their creation.

Though vase figures give us many fine examples of Greek painting, they only hint at the brilliance Greece's artists must have achieved when they worked on a larger scale. The Greeks' records tell us that in the Golden Age, renowned artists decorated public buildings with magnificent frescoes—wall paintings on plaster—showing scenes from their cities' myths and legends. In the Hellenistic Age, Greek artists painted scenes and portraits on immense panels of glass, wood, and marble. Time has erased all the Greek frescoes, and only faded Roman copies remain of a few Hellenistic masterworks. Today we can only guess at the brilliance of an art that once moved the world.

Sculpture

Early Greek sculptors carved wood or molded bronze into stiff, life-size human forms. But in its Golden Age, Greece experienced an artistic revolution that brought its statues to life.

The masterpieces of Greek sculpture seem to do everything

The paintings on this Greek vase show a company of actors preparing for a performance.

but sing. Stone muscles strain and stretch. Faces gently smile or calmly consider. The folds of a gown almost rustle in the breeze. The gods were the sculptors' favorite subjects, but they also shaped perfectly muscled athletes and beautiful women and children. The Greeks sought to make their figures flawless. Only then could their art express the perfect beauty and power of their gods and reflect the wonders of the world the gods created.

Like their pottery and paintings, the Greeks' statues filled their homes and public places. Their art honored their gods and cast glory on their poleis. In later years, though, nearly all Greek bronze sculpture was melted down for use in weapons. Only a few bronze statues, and a few works of marble, escaped the fire and the hand of time. Today they reach across the ages, silent guardians of a dream of ideal beauty.

Architecture

To architecture, as to all their arts, the Greeks brought a sense of grace, balance, and simple perfection. Those qualities shine most clearly in the Greek temples. For it was to the temples honoring their gods and, in turn, their cities, that the Greeks devoted the largest measure of their wealth and genius.

The basic design of the Greek temple remained nearly unchanged for four centuries. The temple was a rectangular building with a porched entrance, its sloping roof held up by columns inside and out. Over time three styles, or orders, developed for carrying out that basic plan: Doric, Ionic, and Corinthian.

The Doric order of architecture emerged in the seventh century B.C.E. on the Greek mainland. Doric columns are thick and powerful. They have no base but are topped with a plain round capital. Most Athenian temples, including the famous Parthenon in Athens, were built in the strong, simple Doric style.

The Ionic order of architecture developed later in the seventh century B.C.E., in the new Ionian colonies across the Aegean. Ionic columns are taller and more slender than Doric; they have a rounded base and a scroll-shaped capital. This elegant, expressive style slowly grew in favor until, in the Golden Age, Doric and Ionic temples stood side by side across Greece. Clever architects even combined the two orders in temples both elegant and majestic.

Lady of Auxerre, *from the seventh century B.C.E., was crafted in the stiff, formal style of early Greek sculpture.*

In Venus of Arles (below), *the fluid, expressive style of Golden Age sculpture brings a Greek goddess to life.*

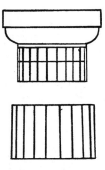

Doric Order

Ionic Order

Corinthian Order

The last and most elaborate of the three architectural orders was Corinthian. First used in the city-state Corinth in the fourth century B.C.E., the Corinthian order adopted the Ionic columns but added capitals intricately carved with delicate leaf patterns. This ornate style was rarely used in the temples of Greece's Golden Age. But centuries later, after Alexander the Great's conquests, Corinthian monuments rose in splendor throughout the Hellenistic world.

Philosophy: The Search for Meaning

How did the world begin? Why do people live, die, think, breathe? Myths of the gods had always answered the Greeks' questions about the world outside and within. But as the Dark Age ended, a new curiosity blossomed. Greeks began to look for logical explanations of the forces that control the world. It was the birth of *philosophia*—"the love of wisdom."

The earliest Greek philosophers pondered the mysteries surrounding the physical world. They searched for natural laws that would explain life, change, death, and the connection between all living things. Later philosophers turned to questions about human emotions and understanding. These Sophists, or "teachers of wisdom," traveled from polis to polis during Greece's Golden Age. Each Sophist had his own philosophy, but all questioned long-held beliefs about religion and morality—what is right and wrong. By challenging the Greeks' ancient traditions, the Sophists stimulated thought and debate across the land, paving the way for a burst of new ideas.

Masters of Thought

The most famous Greek philosopher left no records of his teachings. Everything we know about Socrates (SAH-kruh-teez) comes through the writings of his students. From them comes the picture of a wealthy man who turned his back on money's comforts. In bare feet and his one simple robe, Socrates roamed the roads of Athens using a special teaching style, later called the Socratic method, to challenge all he passed. Asking a question, Socrates would pick apart his student's answer to reveal its errors. Then he

The Erechtheum on Athens's Acropolis, dedicated to several gods, is different from all other Greek temples. Instead of being surrounded by columns, the temple has porches on three sides; the roof of the south porch is held up by a row of graceful maidens.

would ask another question, and another, leading the student to examine his own ideas and reason his way to the truth.

The ultimate truth, in Socrates' philosophy, was that happiness is the highest good people can achieve and knowledge is the only road to happiness. In search of knowledge Socrates questioned everyone and everything. He looked deep into the heart of Athens's faith and traditions. Many Athenians found his endless questions disturbing. Some thought him dangerous. In 399 B.C.E. Socrates was charged with mocking the gods and endangering morality. He refused to give up teaching and was condemned to death.

After Socrates' death many of his loyal students fled Athens. Ten years later one returned. Plato, a gifted poet and playwright, began a series of writings called the *Dialogues*, in which he recalled conversations between Socrates and his students. In time Plato developed his own philosophy and put his ideas into

Socrates' mouth. The influence of Plato's writings has lasted for centuries, for they touched on nearly every subject explored by Western philosophy from his day on.

To further his teachings Plato founded a school called the Academy. This famous place of learning's most notable student was the philosopher Aristotle. Aristotle spent four years in Macedonia as tutor to Greece's future king, the ambitious Alexander. He then returned to Athens and founded the Lyceum, a university patterned on his old master's school.

Aristotle was fascinated by the weather, the stars, the sea, plants and animals, politics, literature, religion, and the human soul. His goal was simply to examine and understand *everything*. His writings covered so broad a field that hardly a branch of ancient science or religion grew without feeling his influence. Over the next twenty centuries Western scholars would honor Aristotle's wisdom by giving him the name "The Philosopher."

Science and Mathematics: The Keys to Mystery

Greek philosophy and science were two plants grown from the same seed. Like its philosophers, ancient Greece's scientists attempted to unlock the mysteries of nature. Over time their studies branched into many different fields. But whether their interests lay in the human body or the stars, these early scientists were all united by a common bond. They were the first seekers of scientific knowledge to use logic to move from the seen to the unseen. They studied what could be touched and observed and then figured out the general principles that rule the physical world—the principles that make the heart pump and the planets revolve. This great leap of reason earned the Greeks fame as the founders of modern science.

Science in the Golden Age

One of the earliest and brightest Greek scientists was Anaxagoras (aa-naak-SAA-guh-ruhs), who lived in the fifth century B.C.E. A student of astronomy—the study of the planets and stars— Anaxagoras challenged the Greeks' ancient belief that the sun was a god and the universe moved at the gods' commands. Through

This fourth-century B.C.E. relief—a work of sculpture in which figures are carved out of the background—shows a physician at work. He treats one patient while another lies waiting for care.

observation and thought, Anaxagoras concluded that the sun was a white-hot rock. He also correctly explained how eclipses occur. Other early Greek astronomers described how the earth rotates on its axis and how the planets revolve around the sun.

The same leap from superstition to science was made by the Greeks in the field of medicine. Hippocrates (hih-PAH-kruh-teez), the father of medicine, believed that illness was the work not of the gods but of physical causes. Disease, he concluded, could be treated or prevented not with magic charms but through proper diet, exercise, and medication. Followers of Hippocrates pledged to help the sick through scientific study and treatment and to follow a code of honorable behavior. Today graduating doctors make the same pledge when they take the Hippocratic oath.

The Golden Age also brought advances in the study of weather, geography, matter, and mathematics. Democritus (dih-MAHkruh-tuhs) proposed that everything is made up of tiny particles that he named atoms. Pythagoras (puh-THAA-guh-ruhs) tried to explain the nature of all things through mathematical principles. He discovered many of the rules on which modern geometry—the mathematics of lines, shapes, and angles—is based and was the first scientist to suggest that the world was round.

An Era of Brilliance

In the Hellenistic Age books and ideas flowed freely through the lands united by Alexander's conquests. For the first time Greeks were able to study the work of scientists from other ancient cultures. Under these fresh influences Greek science made its greatest advances.

The top scientist and inventor of the Hellenistic period was the mathematical genius Archimedes (ahr-kuh-MEED-eez). In the third century B.C.E. Archimedes discovered the principle of the lever and made a famous boast: "Give me a place to stand, and I will move the world." When challenged, he proved his point by using a complicated set of levers and pulleys to single-handedly lift a large ship from water to land.

Other Hellenistic scientists made important discoveries about plants, animals, the human body, the earth, and the universe. Eratosthenes (ehr-uh-TAHS-thuh-neez) drew a map of the world and measured the earth's circumference—the distance all the way around the planet. Theophrastus (thee-uh-FRAAHS-tuhs) described and cataloged every known plant in the world. Other scholars charted the heavens, described earth's orbit, and explained how blood circulates through the human body. It was an age of brilliant and rapid advances. For science, it was one of the ancient world's finest hours.

Government and Society: The Experiment in Democracy

Over the course of a thousand years, ancient Greece moved from the rule of kings to government by nobles to the establishment in late-sixth-century Athens of the world's first democracy.

Every citizen of democratic Athens was automatically a

member of the city's main governing body, the Assembly. Every nine days the Assembly met to decide on laws and public policies such as taxes and building programs. Every citizen had a vote as well as the right to present his opinions before the Assembly.

Demosthenes, a famous fourth-century B.C.E. Athenian patriot, addresses the Assembly.

Athenians also were expected to take turns serving in different government posts.

Ten generals and several high officials or magistrates were elected each year to oversee the Athenian government, but all other posts were filled by lot. These included membership in the Council, a group of five hundred citizens who proposed laws and

35

policies for debate in the Assembly, and the Court, a group of six thousand who acted as jury in cases of murder, theft, and other crimes. The lottery system gave every citizen an equal chance to work in nearly every part of government.

It was the broadest and most equal democracy in history—if you were an Athenian citizen. Yet, out of 315,000 Athenians, only 40,000 belonged to that privileged group. Only free men over the age of twenty-one born to Athenian parents could call themselves citizens. Excluded from political power and rights were all others—all foreigners, women, and slaves.

The Greek Woman

Women played no public role in the Greece that rose to glory. In ancient Crete women had worked as man's equal in the fields and in the arts. In Mycenaean times husbands and wives walked side by side in the streets. But the Golden Age was man's hour. In Athens and the other democratic poleis, women were forbidden to vote, attend school, own property, work in business or the arts, or even appear in public except for occasional veiled visits to relatives or the theater.

The Greek woman's only role in life was to obey her husband, manage his household, and raise their children. With the help of slaves she prepared meals, spun cloth, made the family's clothes and bedding, and kept accounts of the home's goods and expenses. She spent nearly all her life indoors, in the women's quarters at the rear of the house.

By the end of the Golden Age, women were gradually escaping their restrictions. The philosopher Plato welcomed both men and women students to his Academy, and followers of Hippocrates trained many women to become doctors. In the Hellenistic Age, women mingled freely in the streets and made many contributions to philosophy, science, and the arts.

Workingmen and Slaves

Beneath the body of Greek citizens was a large class of foreign immigrants, or *metics*. These were the free workingmen of Athens—the merchants, manufacturers, craftsmen, doctors, lawyers, and teachers. Because one or both of their parents was of

foreign birth, the *metics* were denied the political rights of citizens. But their contributions and skills were respected, and many *metics* earned great riches.

Beneath the *metics* were the slaves. Ironically, slavery was one of the key reasons behind the vitality of Greek democracy. The Greek citizen had a wife to run his household and slaves to do his manual work. That left him free to devote his life to serving his city's government.

In the Golden Age one out of every three Athenians was a slave. Most were foreigners who had been captured in wars or pirate raids. These unfortunate men and women were auctioned off for prices ranging from the equivalents of $50 to $1,000, depend-

Upper-class Greek women relax in a fifth-century B.C.E. painting. Their tunics, or chitons, are made of finely spun wool or linen, and their hair is worn fashionably long, held up in the back by a net and ribbons.

Two women play knuckle-bones, a favorite game of the ancient Greeks. It was played like jacks, with pieces made from the anklebones of small animals.

ing on their skills. Even the poorest Greek citizen or *metic* owned at least one slave, and rich households might have as many as fifty.

Women slaves worked at chores in the Greek home. Men labored in silver mines or rock quarries or worked beside their masters in their homes, fields, businesses, or workshops. Some slaves were treated cruelly. In general, though, the Greeks were kinder masters than most other ancient peoples. Greek law forbade a master from killing his slave. Some slave owners rewarded loyal workers by paying them wages or by allowing the slave to live and work on his own in return for a share of his earnings. If a slave saved enough money, he could buy his freedom.

A few Greeks spoke out against slavery, but throughout Greek history the great majority accepted it without question. No matter how contradictory it seems, the Greeks saw slavery as an essential part of their society's achievements under democracy.

IF YOU LIVED IN ANCIENT GREECE

If you had been born during the Golden Age of Greece, your way of life would have been determined by the facts of your birth—whether you were a girl or a boy; free or slave; wealthy or poor; Athenian, Spartan, or Ionian colonist. With this chart you can trace the course your life might have taken as a citizen of ancient Greece's greatest city-state.

You were born in Athens. . . .

As a Boy . . .

As a Girl . . .

You live in a simple one-story house with about ten rooms and a central courtyard. You have many toys, including a wagon, balls, kites, and clay soldiers or dolls. You don't see your father much but are well cared for by your mother and the family's nursery slaves.

At age 6 you begin school. From sunrise to sunset you go to a private schoolmaster who teaches you and several other boys reading, writing, poetry, arithmetic, drawing, painting, music, and sports. You learn to recite from memory all 26,000 lines of Homer's *Iliad* and *Odyssey* and to play the lyre and the double-pipes.

At age 14 or 16 your schooling in letters ends, but physical training picks up. You work out every day at the public gymnasium, wrestling, playing ball, running, and learning to toss the javelin.

At age 18 you leave home to begin two years of military service, learning the art of war and good citizenship. You debate laws in a junior Assembly. At 19, you are assigned to patrol your city's borders.

At age 21 you are an adult and a full citizen. You live an active life. You shop and discuss philosophy, science, and art in the agora (AH-guh-rah), or central marketplace; debate in the Assembly; keep fit in the gymnasium; and attend the theater, religious festivals, and athletic contests. Around age 30, you marry. You love your family but spend little time at home.

At age 6 your schooling begins. You are educated at home by your mother and nurses, who teach you reading, writing, arithmetic, and the skills you'll need to please a husband and run a home. You learn to sing and play an instrument and spend many hours spinning, weaving, and embroidering.

At age 14 or 15 you marry the man your father chooses, usually someone about twice your age. Your father gives you a dowry of money, cloth, and slaves to take with you to your husband's home.

As wife and mother, you spend your days quietly but actively at home. You are responsible for producing everything your family eats and wears and are respected for the skill with which you manage your household.

If your husband dies before you, his property passes to your sons, but you keep your dowry. Unless your husband's will chooses another husband for you, you must return to the care of your father or another male relative.

Athenian tradition demands that the young respect the elderly, and law commands that your sons support you in your old age. When you die, your body is bathed in perfumed oils and dressed in fine clothes. You are buried in a stone tomb with food and drink for your soul's journey to the underworld.

CHAPTER THREE

THE GLORIOUS GODS

The early Greeks imagined wondrous beings in every corner of the earth, sea, and sky. Those beings made the ground shake and the seasons change. They made people fall in love, suffer illness, give birth, and die. They were divine explanations for every blessing and every disaster.

By Homer's day thousands of gods and goddesses crowded Greek religion. All had their own fascinating stories, or *mythos,* which explained their powers and history. Homer imposed order on this magnificent riot of separate, sometimes contradictory myths. His epic poems explained relationships between the gods—who was father, sister, son. He gave each god a title and specific areas of responsibility: god of the sea, god of war. He gave his gods very human personalities. And Homer's writings raised one particular set of divinities above all others. These were the gods who were said to live in a golden palace atop Greece's highest mountain, Mount Olympus. Through the poems of Homer and another famous eighth-century B.C.E. epic poet, Hesiod, the Olympian gods became the heart and majesty of Greek religion.

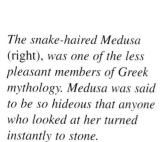

The snake-haired Medusa (right), *was one of the less pleasant members of Greek mythology. Medusa was said to be so hideous that anyone who looked at her turned instantly to stone.*

The Twelve Olympians

On a mountain so high that no human could climb it dwelt the all-powerful Olympians. They looked like humans, only taller, handsomer, more beautiful. They behaved like humans— they quarreled, grew jealous, played tricks, fell in love. They were immortal, so they lived forever. But they took great interest in the world of mortals below them.

The Children of Cronus

Zeus

The king of all the gods carried a thunderbolt and was worshiped as god of the weather, law, property, liberty, and nearly every other part of life. Zeus's father was Cronus, lord of the universe; his mother was Rhea, or Mother Earth. To protect his supremacy Cronus had swallowed his first five children. But Rhea saved her sixth child, Zeus, by hiding him in a cave and giving Cronus a

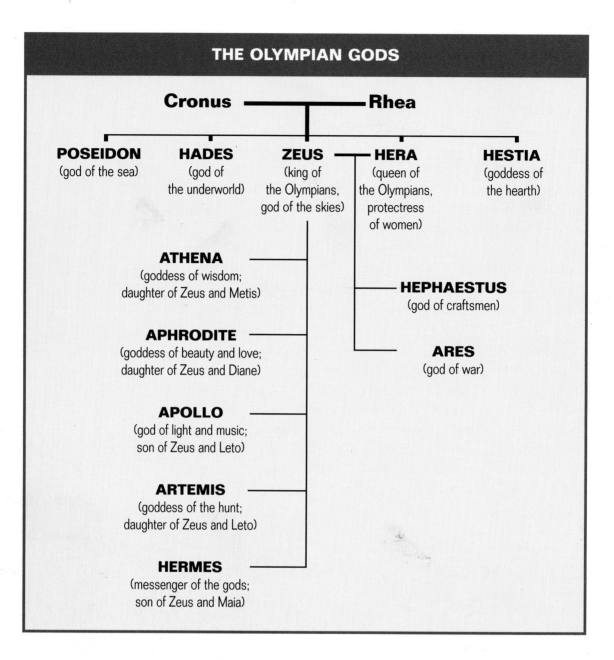

THE OLYMPIAN GODS

Cronus ———————— **Rhea**

POSEIDON
(god of the sea)

HADES
(god of
the underworld)

ZEUS
(king of
the Olympians,
god of the skies)

HERA
(queen of
the Olympians,
protectress
of women)

HESTIA
(goddess of
the hearth)

ATHENA
(goddess of wisdom;
daughter of Zeus and Metis)

HEPHAESTUS
(god of craftsmen)

APHRODITE
(goddess of beauty and love;
daughter of Zeus and Diane)

ARES
(god of war)

APOLLO
(god of light and music;
son of Zeus and Leto)

ARTEMIS
(goddess of the hunt;
daughter of Zeus and Leto)

HERMES
(messenger of the gods;
son of Zeus and Maia)

stone wrapped in baby clothes to swallow instead. When Zeus grew into a powerful god, Rhea helped him trick Cronus into drinking a magic potion that made him throw up his other five children. Cronus fled, and Zeus became lord of the universe. He chose to share his power with his brothers. Poseidon (poh-SAI-duhn) received rule of the sea, Hades (HAY-deez) rule of the underworld (the land of the dead), and Zeus kept the heavens and earth. Two of Zeus's sisters, Hestia and Hera, also joined him on the thrones of Mount Olympus. His third sister, Demeter, goddess of the harvest, lived on earth, tending her gardens.

Poseidon

The god of the sea was moody and violent. He carried a three-pointed spear, or trident, and raced the waves in a chariot pulled by a team of white horses. When Poseidon's trident struck the sea, the waters shook and split open. The special god of sailors, Poseidon was also worshiped as the god of earthquakes and of horses, which he had created in the image of a breaking wave.

Hades

"Unseen," or Hades, was the Greeks' name for both the god of the underworld and the fearsome place itself. When a person died, his soul journeyed far below ground to the River Styx (STIHKS). He was rowed across the river's black waters by the grim ferryman Charon (KAAR-uhn). On the other side was a three-headed dog that let dead souls enter Hades but never leave again. Most souls spent eternity as mindless shadows wandering aimlessly through Hades' dark kingdom. A very few—the most heroic of men—were allowed to pass on to the Elysian (ih-LEE-zhuhn) Fields, a paradise of eternal happiness.

Hera

Zeus's sister Hera was the most important of his many wives. She was worshiped as the protectress of women and marriage. A beautiful and jealous queen, Hera spent most of her time spying on her husband. Once, Zeus tried to hide the pretty maiden Io from his wife by changing the girl into a little white cow. Hera was not fooled. Admiring the cow, she begged Zeus to let her have it. Then she tied Io to a tree and left her one-hundred-eyed servant Argus as guard. Zeus rescued Io by sending his son Hermes to charm Argus to sleep and cut off his head. The furious Hera sent a stinging fly that chased the little cow all the way to Egypt. Then she honored the memory of her servant by placing his many eyes on the tail of her favorite bird, the peacock.

On this fifth-century B.C.E. painted wine cup, Hera takes a dignified pose suited to her role as queen of the Olympians.

Hestia

The goddess of the hearth or fireplace was the only Olympian who had no throne. The gentlest of the divinities, she sat tending the sacred fire in the Olympian palace hall. Hestia was widely worshiped as a symbol of the value of home and family. Every polis honored her in the sacred fire that burned day and night in its public hearth.

The Children of Zeus

Zeus had many children, but only seven sat on golden thrones in the palace on Mount Olympus.

Athena

The name of the daughter of Zeus and Metis means "wisdom." Zeus had been warned that if Metis had a son, the child would one day overthrow him. So when Metis became pregnant, Zeus swallowed her whole. Metis's growing infant traveled to Zeus's head and months later was born out of his skull, fully grown and dressed in armor. Athena was worshiped as the goddess of wisdom, of arts and crafts, and of war and peace. The patron goddess of Athens, she watched over the city from her magnificent temple, the Parthenon.

Aphrodite

The goddess of love and beauty was as vain as she was beautiful. Aphrodite played a role in starting the Trojan War. All the goddesses had been invited to a party except one—Eris, the spirit of discord, or conflict. The spiteful Eris tossed the invited guests a golden apple inscribed with the words *For the Fairest.* Immediately, Hera, Athena, and Aphrodite all claimed the apple. To settle their dispute, Zeus sent the goddesses to the handsomest man on earth, Paris, son of the king of Troy. Each goddess promised Paris a great prize if he would judge her the fairest. Hera promised wealth and power, Athena promised wisdom, and Aphrodite offered Paris the most beautiful woman in the world. Paris presented the apple to Aphrodite. She rewarded him with Helen, the Mycenaean queen whose abduction to Troy set off the Trojan War.

Apollo

Second only to Zeus in power, Apollo was worshiped as the god of light, music, poetry, art, healing, and prophecy. A wise and noble god, he took over the sacred shrine of Delphi on the slopes of Mount Parnassus by slaying its dragon guardian. From then on, when people came to Delphi with questions about their future, Apollo would whisper the answers to the priestess who tended his shrine. A constant stream of visitors from all over the Greek world led their lives by the words of the famous shrine at Delphi.

Artemis

Apollo's twin sister was the goddess of the hunt. Mistress of all wild things, she rode through the woods in a silver chariot pulled by a team of deer with golden antlers. Forever unmarried and young, Artemis was also worshiped as the protectress of children.

The wise and powerful young Apollo, god of light, healing, and the arts, was one of the most widely worshiped Greek divinities.

Ares (AAR-eez)

This son of Zeus and Hera was the god of war. Unlike Athena, the protectress of people who waged just and righteous wars, bloodthirsty Ares loved war for its own sake. In the Trojan War, Athena sided with the Greeks, but Ares swung his dreadful sword alongside the Trojans.

Hephaestus (hih-FEHS-tuhs)

Ares' brother was the god of craftsmen and fire. Because he was born with a deformed leg, Hera tossed him from Olympus. Years later Hephaestus returned, and his kind and gentle ways made him a favorite among the gods. Often, when Zeus and Hera argued, Hephaestus tried to make peace. Once this so enraged Zeus that he hurled his son to earth again. The fall broke Hephaestus's ankle, and from then on he hobbled about on legs too weak to hold him. But Hephaestus had strong arms and talented hands. He crafted marvelous thrones, chariots, and even magic silver-tongued robots. Sometimes he worked at fiery forges deep inside volcanoes. Then the clang of his hammers shook the earth and sparks flew from the mountaintops.

Hermes (HUHR-meez)

This was the merry young god of shepherds, travelers, and thieves. A bright and cunning infant, he invented the lyre on the afternoon of his birth. Then he crept from his cradle and rounded up fifty of Apollo's snow-white cattle. When Apollo came thundering in search of the thief, he found an infant with wide, innocent eyes. Grabbing his little brother, Apollo hauled him to Olympus, where Zeus shook with laughter at his baby son's cleverness. Zeus made Hermes the messenger of the gods and gave him a golden cap and sandals with wings. As a messenger for Hades, Hermes guided the souls of the dead to the underworld.

The youthful god Hermes holds an even younger Dionysus, the god of wine who became so popular that, in time, a place was found for him on Mount Olympus.

The Lesser Gods

Below the supreme Olympians were thousands of minor gods. Each craft and art that the Greeks practiced had its own patron god, every object or force of nature its own spirit. Besides the gods there were other types of deities—demigods, nymphs, demons. Even the epic poet Hesiod, who wrote a long catalog of the Greek divinities, confessed it was impossible for anyone to remember all their names.

Here are just a few members of the Greeks' divine multitude:

THE GODS GO ROMAN

The Romans came to Greece with their own ancient gods, but Roman mythology lacked the excitement of the Greek tales. So the Romans gradually attached the colorful Greek stories to their own gods' names. Their sky god Jupiter starred in the Greek myths about Zeus, their god of water in Poseidon's stories. Today we know the Greek gods better by the names the Romans gave them.

Greek	Roman (Latin)
Zeus	Jupiter
Poseidon	Neptune
Hades	Pluto
Hera	Juno
Hestia	Vesta
Athena	Minerva
Aphrodite	Venus
Apollo	Apollo*
Artemis	Diana
Ares	Mars
Hephaestus	Vulcan
Hermes	Mercury

* The Romans had no god like Apollo, so they borrowed his name along with his stories.

The Fates
These three goddesses decided the length of a mortal's life. For each person born, one Fate spun a thread, the second measured its length, and the third cut it at the moment of death.

The Gorgons
The three horrible Gorgon sisters had birds' bodies, women's heads, and hair made of living snakes. Any mortal who looked at these repulsive monsters turned to stone. The most famous Gorgon was Medusa, mother of a beautiful winged horse called Pegasus.

The Graces
Goddesses of beauty, the three Graces served Aphrodite and watched over all celebrations of marriage.

The Harpies
These two wicked wind spirits swooped down on men's feasts and snatched their food.

The Hours
Daughters of Zeus and goddesses of nature, the Hours brought the changing seasons. In early mythology, three Hours reflected nature's cycles of sprouting, growth, and ripeness. Later

Greeks added a fourth sister to the myths, and the four Hours became the spirits of the four seasons.

The Muses

Nine Muses, goddesses of the arts, inspired writers, musicians, and scientists. Greek philosophers dedicated their academies to the Muses; these places of learning came to be called *museums*.

Nymphs

These fairylike goddesses dwelt everywhere in nature. There were nymphs of springs and pools, rivers, the sea, mountains, clouds, and woodlands.

Satyrs (SAY-tuhrz)

Brothers of the nymphs and spirits of wildlife, the satyrs had goats' legs and hooves, pointed ears, and horns. Their master was Pan, god of nature. Pan played heavenly music on shepherd's pipes, but in a mischievous mood he might infect animals and people with a wild fear called *panic*.

Three of the Muses, Greek guardians of the arts, hold the symbols of their special areas of protection.

Centaurs

These wild, vulgar creatures were men from head to waist and horses from the waist down.

Demigods

There were also mortals who were more powerful than ordinary humans but less powerful than gods. Demigods had one divine parent and one human parent, and they often became immortal after death. The most famous demigod was Dionysus (die-uh-NYE-suhs), god of wine, who died each fall and was reborn again each spring. Dionysus was such a popular god that in time he took his own throne on Mount Olympus. Another demigod was Asclepius (uh-SKLEE-pee-uhs), son of Apollo and the mortal princess Coronis. Asclepius was a doctor so skilled he could bring the dead back to life. When Hades complained about this to Zeus, the king of gods killed Asclepius with a thunderbolt. Asclepius became the god of medicine and went to live among the stars.

Myths and Mysteries

Greek mythology answered nearly every question about nature and life. Here are three ancient myths that the Greeks invented to explain our mysterious world.

Man's Creation and the Gift of Fire

In the beginning the Olympians ruled over an empty world. So Zeus gave the job of creating living creatures to two brothers, Epimetheus and Prometheus. Epimetheus made many animals, but Prometheus made only one—man. Carefully he molded mud into the shape of a god. His creation would not crawl like the other creatures but would walk proud and upright. By the time Prometheus was done, though, his brother had used up all the gods' best gifts—speed, keen sight, flight—on the other animals. Nothing was left for Prometheus's new creature, not even fur to keep him warm. So Prometheus sneaked into Olympus and stole an ember from the chariot of the sun. Then, descending to earth, he gave the gift of fire to man.

Pandora's Box, or the Roots of Evil

Zeus was furious at Prometheus for stealing the gods' sacred fire—and at man for accepting Prometheus's gift. So he crafted a new creature like man but smaller and more beautiful. Zeus named the first woman Pandora. He gave her a locked wooden box, warned her never to open it, and sent her to live on earth. For days the box preyed on Pandora's mind. Finally curiosity overcame her. She turned the key. The lid flew open, and out raced a thousand evils—Disease, Pain, Cruelty, Madness, War, Death. Pandora slammed the lid shut, but it was too late. Only one thing saved man from total despair at the terrible gifts Pandora had let loose. Among the evils, Prometheus had secretly placed a tiny creature called Hope.

Prometheus flees Mount Olympus with the precious gift of fire, in a painting by the seventeenth-century painter Jan Cossiers.

Persephone and the Origin of the Seasons

In the early days the earth always bloomed. The goddess of the harvest, Demeter, tended the fruit trees and filled the wheat ears with grain. By her side as she worked was her daughter Persephone (puhr-SEH-fuh-nee), a girl so graceful and sunny that even Hades deep beneath the ground took notice. Harnessing his chariot, the grim god thundered to earth, grabbed Persephone, and dragged her down to his kingdom. Demeter begged for Zeus's help, and the king of gods ordered Hades to let Persephone go. But Hades loved the bright girl and could not bear to lose her. So he tricked her into eating six seeds from a juicy red pomegranate. Persephone had tasted the food of the dead, unknowingly condemning herself to returning to the dark god's kingdom. For six months each year, Persephone must sit beside Hades as queen of the land of shadows. Demeter weeps, and the earth withers and dies. Then Persephone returns to the light, Demeter rejoices, and the earth blossoms again.

Women joyfully offer the first fruits of the harvest to Demeter, goddess of earth's fertility. Harvest festivals were one way the Greeks honored their gods and asked for continued protection and favor.

The Ways of Worship

The Greek gods, with their very human personalities and behavior, were hardly examples of good conduct. In fact there were no rules of proper conduct in Greek religion. There was no creed, or specific set of religious beliefs, either. Instead all Greeks were free to believe what they wanted and behave as they thought best, as long as they joined in the official ceremonies of worship.

Worship was a way to win the favor of the all-powerful gods. Good luck, health, and success in love, business, or war were the rewards of those who pleased the gods. But the Greek who somehow provoked a god's anger could expect only disaster.

The Greeks worshiped at hearths in their homes, their city halls, their temples, and their shrines. In the home the family offered prayers and food or wine to their favorite god. In the temples (the polis's home for its patron god) and the shrines (dedicated to one special god but open to Greeks from all poleis) worship ceremonies were more elaborate. A grand procession to the sacred site was followed by chanting, prayers, music, and dance. The Greeks might offer the gods valued possessions like weapons or pottery, and sacrifice an animal, perhaps a bull, sheep, or pig. Every word and movement of the ceremony followed ancient custom, preserved in the city's sacred books.

The poleis also held special religious festivals several times a year. Along with ceremonies honoring a city's patron god, festivals featured athletic contests. Many of these contests were panhellenic—Greeks from every polis were allowed to compete. The most famous panhellenic festival was held at Olympia, the center for worship of Zeus. Every four years thousands of Greeks gathered to cheer the athletes at these Olympic Games.

Death of the Immortals

When Philip of Macedonia attacked the poleis, prayers and the smoke of sacrificial fires rose all across Greece. But Philip conquered, and Alexander the Great ruled. The Greeks began to turn away from the gods who had proved helpless to defend them.

Superstitions and strange religious cults multiplied across Alexander's empire. Egyptian and Middle Eastern gods blended with Greek divinities and were worshiped in Greek temples. A handful of these new gods gradually displaced all the others. Then worship of one central god began to replace the worship of many. The new trend paved the way for the Greeks' embrace of a single god, at the birth of Christianity.

The clouds of mystery surrounding Mount Olympus had parted. The ancient Greek religion had died but the Greek gods lived on. In the enchanted world of their mythology, they will always be immortal.

CHAPTER FOUR

THE MYTHS WORK THEIR MAGIC

The mythology of ancient Greece is more than the unforgettable stories of its gods. The imaginative Greeks invented hundreds of tales about mortal men, too. There was Perseus, slayer of the snake-haired Gorgon; Heracles (HEHR-uh-kleez), performer of twelve superhuman labors; Theseus, destroyer of the monstrous Minotaur; Jason, seeker of the Golden Fleece. These men of unusual strength and bravery were called heroes. In their myths they lived in an earlier age, a Heroic Age when men were nobler and closer to the gods.

The legendary heroes overcame giant obstacles to perform wondrous deeds. Like all mortals, they one day died. But like the gods, they were worshiped in cults scattered throughout Greece, and their deeds were celebrated in poetry and art. Together, the myths of gods and men touched the lives of all Greeks, shaping and enlightening their culture.

Mythology's Many Uses

Myths of gods and heroes delighted Greek listeners, but these tales were more than good entertainment. For the ancient Greeks, mythology was history, example, and inspiration.

During the Dark Age, when the Greek people scattered and the roots of their

PERSEUS AND THE GORGON

Perseus was the son of Zeus and the beautiful princess Danaë (DAA-nuh-ee). An evil king tried to force Danaë to marry him, but Perseus protected her. So the king plotted to get rid of Perseus by ordering him to cut off the head of Medusa.

Medusa was one of the Gorgons, the horrible sisters whose very looks turned people to stone. But the gods helped Zeus's son in his dangerous mission. They gave him winged sandals, a polished silver shield, a helmet of invisibility, and a mighty sword. Wearing the sandals, Perseus flew to the island of the Gorgons. He saw Medusa but was not turned to stone, for he only looked at her reflection in the gods' gleaming shield. Invisible in his magic helmet, Perseus swooped down and cut off Medusa's head.

When Perseus returned home and announced his success, the evil king laughed in disbelief. The hero pulled out Medusa's head and turned the king to stone. Then Perseus founded a new kingdom in the splendid walled city of Mycenae.

culture seemed to vanish, myths kept that culture alive. The epic songs created by traveling minstrels preserved memories of past glories. Many of the human heroes of these epics were once flesh-and-blood men who had played important roles in Minoan and Mycenaean history. With each retelling, however, the tales of their lives became more fantastic. The minstrels entertained their audiences by weaving imaginative new details into the old stories. They transformed ordinary beasts into frightful

Riding the beautiful winged horse Pegasus, the hero Perseus bears proof of his victory over snake-haired Medusa.

monsters, and they gave their heroes superhuman powers and magic weapons to conquer their enemies.

Greece's kings, nobles, and city leaders encouraged the minstrels to improve on history. Like anyone, the leaders enjoyed an exciting action story. They also enjoyed the glory of claiming heroic ancestors, especially ancestors related to the gods. So the imaginative poets added lines that let the kings of Thebes trace their parentage back to Zeus and turned the nobles of Athens into distant sons of heroic King Theseus.

By Homer's day thousands of versions of the heroic myths were sung across Greece. We've seen how Homer made order from the chaos of the gods' myths. At the same time he organized the heroic tales. The *Iliad* and the *Odyssey* established relationships among the heroes and gods—who were father and son, friend and foe, mortal man and divine protector. Homer's epics also gave the ancient tales a simple moral code. His heroes might be selfish and even cruel at times, but they were always loyal to their friends and family, true to their word, and courageous in their goals and their deeds.

The legends recorded by Homer and the poets who followed him re-created a history of proud, almost godly achievements. They held up an example of ideal conduct—by filling his life with the pursuit of noble goals, the Greek might find honor and glory. These tales of gods and men became the heart not only of the Greeks' religion but of their history and moral teachings, too.

Mythology in the Arts

Nearly every work of Greek literature and art revolved around the world of mythology.

Gods and heroes were central to Homer's epics, and their stories continued in the dramas written by Greece's playwrights. The most famous play by Aeschylus, *Prometheus Bound,* is the story of Zeus's revenge on the god who gave man fire. From the playwright Sophocles came *Oedipus* (EH-duh-puhs), a tragedy based on the myth of a king condemned by fate to murder his father and marry his mother. Euripides' *Medea* turned the legend of Jason and the Golden Fleece into a powerful drama of love and betrayal.

In paintings, too, the Greek myths came to life. Gleaming gods and heroes danced in endless circles around the sides of fine Greek pottery. The Olympians, the Trojan War, and the adventures of Jason, Heracles, and Theseus were among the potters' favorite themes. The vast Golden Age frescoes often showed scenes from heroic mythology. One of the most famous frescoes, the *Sack of Troy,* filled the walls of an Athenian market building with the victors and victims of the Trojan War.

In its sculpture, Greece captured the perfection of its gods and the godlike grace of its heroes. Mighty Zeus hurled his thunderbolt. Athena rose in majesty to guard her city. Heracles held up the sky for the god Atlas. Most Greek sculpture was created for

Prometheus Bound, *by the seventeenth-century Flemish master Peter Paul Rubens. According to mythology, Prometheus's punishment for giving fire to man was to be chained for eternity to a mountain, where he was attacked each day by a fierce eagle.*

the temples. Statues were housed within a temple's sacred chambers, and images were carved into its roof, walls, and columns. The most famous temple statue was the Zeus of Olympia. Sixty feet tall and carved from ivory and gold, the idol even inspired its own mythology. When the sculptor was finished, poets said, he begged for a sign of heaven's approval, and a bolt of lightning struck the stone before the golden god's feet.

The decorative sculpture that graced Greek temples often showed scenes from mythology and legends. This stone carving topped the columns of a temple to Apollo. It depicts a battle between men and centaurs, mythical half-man, half-horse creatures.

Mythology in Everyday Life

Mythology's many roles—preserving history, teaching morality, inspiring art—combined to urge ancient Greece to cultural triumphs. It was in its first role, however, as sourcebook for religion, that myth had its greatest impact on the average Greek's daily life.

The myths said divine spirits lived in every part of the earth and sky, so the Greek people worshiped their gods everywhere. They offered prayers and gifts in the temples, on mountaintops, before sacred caves, above cracks in the earth, and at their homes' sacred hearths. Many Greeks were superstitious. They believed not only in the myths about the Olympians and heroes but also in tales of demons, monsters, and evil spirits. Only magic rituals could hold off these dark powers.

THESEUS AND THE MINOTAUR

When King Minos of Crete defeated Athens in war, he demanded a terrible payment. Each year Athens must send seven young boys and seven maidens to be fed to Crete's monstrous Minotaur. Half man, half bull, the Minotaur lived beneath Minos's palace in a maze of halls and rooms called the Labyrinth.

To save his kingdom, King Aegeus (ih-JEE-uhs) of Athens agreed to Minos's demands. But his brave son Theseus vowed to put an end to the dreadful sacrifices. Theseus volunteered to join the victims on the next ship to Crete. When he arrived in Crete, King Minos's daughter Ariadne (aar-ee-AAD-nee) fell in love with him. That night Ariadne told Theseus a secret. No one could escape from the Labyrinth's twisting paths, so the Minotaur simply waited until its victims grew hungry and exhausted, then easily overcame and devoured them. Ariadne gave Theseus a sword and a ball of thread. She waited outside the Labyrinth, holding one end of the thread, while Theseus entered the maze, sneaked up on the Minotaur, killed it, and followed the thread back to freedom.

The Athenians joyfully headed home. But in his eagerness, Theseus forgot that he had promised his father he would change the ship's black sails for white ones to signal his safe return. Watching high on a clifftop, King Aegeus saw the black sails and believed his son was dead. Aegeus threw himself into the sea that has ever after been called the Aegean. Theseus became king of Athens and ruled for many years in kindness, courage, and wisdom.

No careful man cut down a tree before begging forgiveness from the wood nymph who dwelt in it. Special oils and prayers protected travelers from the goddess who lurked at crossroads when the moon was down. Magic water and cleansing ceremonies chased the demons who caused sickness and insanity. The Greeks even took their superstitions with them to the grave. A coin was placed beneath the tongue of a dead person to pay the ferryman for passage across the River Styx.

So many spirits inhabited the Greek world that it was hard to know how to please them all. Many Greeks sought guidance from the gods themselves, at shrines called oracles. A man unsure how to act in a situation affecting his future could ask a god's advice through the priests and priestess of an oracle. The answer to his question would most likely be given in the form of a riddle

The superhuman strength of Heracles was a favorite theme of Greek and Roman paintings, pottery, and sculpture. In this Roman statue, the hero is shown with a lion's head and skin.

THE TWELVE LABORS OF HERACLES

Heracles—to the Romans, Hercules—was the strongest man ever born. Zeus was his father and the mortal princess Alemena was his mother. Hera, always jealous, vowed to destroy Heracles. She struck him with madness, and in a blind rage he murdered six of his children. To pay for his crime he became a slave to a king who ordered him to perform twelve nearly impossible tasks.

Heracles' labors included killing or capturing many monsters that terrorized the kingdom. The hero even journeyed to Hades and stole the three-headed dog that guarded its borders. In performing other feats of courage and strength, he moved mountains and changed the course of rivers. For his final labor he was commanded to steal three golden apples from Hera's garden. That was something even Heracles did not dare. So he asked the god Atlas for help. Atlas had been condemned to hold up the sky forever, but Heracles offered to take the burden from him while Atlas picked the apples. When Atlas returned, though, he was reluctant to take back the sky's crushing weight. So Heracles talked Atlas into holding the sky for just a minute while he padded his own shoulders to make the load more bearable. Then Heracles snatched up the golden apples, ran off as fast as he could, and, with his labors done, earned his freedom.

JASON AND THE GOLDEN FLEECE

Jason was the son of a good king, but when the king's brother, Pelias, seized the throne, young Jason was sent to live in a mountain cave. There he grew to be a brave and handsome man. When he was grown, Jason left the cave to reclaim his father's kingdom.

The wicked Pelias promised to give up the throne if Jason would perform a heroic deed. He must bring back the precious coat of a magic golden ram. The ram's Golden Fleece hung in the kingdom of Colchis (KAHL-kuhs), guarded by an ever-wakeful dragon.

Jason built a magnificent ship, the *Argo,* and set sail with a crew of fifty heroes. The Argonauts had many adventures. They rescued a starving king from the Harpies, who kept stealing his meals. They rowed like the wind to escape the Clashing Rocks, two huge boulders that crushed all ships that tried to pass between them. They survived storms, giant warriors, and pirates. Finally, they reached Colchis.

The cruel king of Colchis hated foreigners. He threatened to kill the Argonauts unless Jason completed an impossible task. The hero had to harness the king's fire-breathing bulls and plant a field with magical dragon-tooth seeds. Each tooth he planted would grow instantly into an armed warrior. With the help of Medea, the king's daughter and a powerful sorceress, Jason succeeded in the task. Then Medea enchanted the dragon guarding the Golden Fleece, and Jason claimed his prize. Together Jason and Medea fled to the *Argo,* and the heroes set sail for home.

The journey was full of dangers, but with the gods' help, the Argonauts reached Greece at last. Wicked Pelias refused to keep his promise and return the throne, so Medea used her magic to destroy him. But Jason soon forgot how much he owed Medea. He asked the sorceress to leave him so he could marry a lovely young princess. Enraged, Medea sent Jason's new bride a wedding gift—an enchanted gown. When the princess put on the gown, she burst into flames. The palace burned to the ground, and Medea flew off into the black smoke on a chariot pulled by serpents. Jason spent his final days miserable and alone. When he died, the Golden Fleece was hung in Apollo's shrine at Delphi as a reminder of his daring deeds.

that could be interpreted in many different ways. This made the god correct no matter what happened. Once, a king asked the famous oracle of Delphi if he should invade a foreign land. The oracle answered that if he invaded, he would destroy a great empire. The king attacked and was defeated—thus destroying his own empire.

Oracles and superstitions were the darker side of Greek

religion. Most worship was full of light and gladness. The gods were mighty, the heroes were noble, and people praised and welcomed them. Happiest of all forms of worship were the religious festivals. The calendar of Athens was crowded with more than one hundred festivals a year. The most popular was the Panathenaea (pan-ath-uh-NAY-uh). This four-day party of songs, costumes, contests, and feasts ended with a colorful pro-

Greek festivals were joyous occasions filled with music, dancing, and feasts, as this nineteenth-century painting shows.

cession to the Acropolis, where a magnificent new gown was pre-sented to the goddess Athena. In such celebrations, the religion inspired by the myths in turn inspired joy, beauty, and pride in the land blessed by the gods.

63

CHAPTER FIVE

THE LASTING LIGHT

When Philip II's armies marched south from Macedonia, it was the beginning of the end for Greek freedom. But ancient Greece's influence on world culture and thought had just begun.

Philip's son Alexander the Great spread Greek culture across a vast empire. After Alexander's death Greek influence continued to grow. From mainland Greece south to Egypt and as far east as India, Greek became the common language of government, education, and trade. Greek scientists studied and taught in the cities Alexander had founded. Sculptors and artists left the declining

Ancient Greek tombs on the coast of present-day Turkey

poleis and inspired a new school of Eastern art based on Greek techniques and styles. Greek architecture, too, transformed the Eastern cities. From Egypt to India new buildings rose like beautifully wrapped packages, blending the simple grace of Greek temple design with the rich adornments of the East.

The Torch Passes

Roman conquest in 86 B.C.E. brought Greece's influence to an even larger world. The Romans admired and copied Greek customs, literature, and art. Their writers imitated the style and topics of Greece's poets and playwrights. Their artists created images of Roman rulers in the Greek style and made marble copies of many of the Greeks' sculptural masterpieces. Roman architects designed public buildings modeled after Greek temples. And the leaders of the Roman Empire borrowed ideas from the laws and government of the poleis. As the Roman Empire continued to expand, all these different strands of Greek culture traveled across the Mediterranean world to southern Europe, northern Africa, and the Middle East.

This mosaic from the second century C.E. shows theater masks like those used in ancient Greece. They were still a part of drama performances centuries after the fall of Athens.

In the fifth century C.E. the Roman Empire itself was conquered. By now the glory days of ancient Greece were a distant memory, and once-mighty Athens lay crumbling. But even the fall of Rome and the ruin of the city-states could not conquer the Greek spirit. Through the new rulers of Rome's old kingdoms and through invaders who paused to sample the riches of those kingdoms on their journeys to distant lands, Greek culture continued to flow across the world.

The Byzantines, rulers of the eastern half of the old Roman Empire, spread a blend of Greek and Asian influences east across Asia and west to Europe. Arab invaders carried Arabic translations of works by Greek scientists and philosophers west on their conquests of northern Africa and Spain. For a thousand years after the fall of Rome, Europe's philosophers explained the world

The statue known as the Laocoön—a Roman copy of a lost Greek original—was found buried in a vineyard in Rome in 1506. The rediscovery inspired a new power and expressiveness in European art. The statue portrays the horrible death of the priest Laocoön and his sons, characters from the Iliad *who were strangled by serpents after warning people against the Trojan horse.*

in terms laid down by Aristotle, and its geographers relied on ancient Greek maps.

Then, in the fourteenth century C.E., Italian scholars and artists began an intensive study of the ancient Greek and Roman civilizations. Supported by the ruling families of Italy's largest cities and aided by the fifteenth-century invention of printing, they spread the ideals of Greek culture throughout Europe. Byzantine scholars fleeing wars in the east settled in Italy, adding their knowledge to the growing cultural movement that came to be called the Renaissance.

This period of brilliant accomplishments in art, literature, and learning saw the *renaissance,* or "rebirth," of Greek ideas and styles. Many newly discovered writings of Homer, Plato, and other Greek masters were translated into Latin for European readers. Scholars also found ancient Roman versions of Greek writings, which they read with new interest. Archaeologists explored Athens and brought back lost statues and sketches of ruined temples. In a fever of admiration European sculptors, architects, poets, dramatists, and philosophers studied and imitated the Greek master-works. Even the gods were reborn—ancient Greece's mythology became so familiar to Europeans that many named their children after Greek and Roman heroes.

The Renaissance was a time of exploration and colonization, too. In each new colony they established, from Africa to Asia to the Americas, the Europeans planted the seeds of the rediscovered Greek culture. In time the colonies became new nations, scattered around the globe. And that is how the spirit of ancient Greece passed from one culture to the next, down through the centuries, to touch our lives today.

The Living Greeks

In our modern world the civilization of ancient Greece seems very old and far away. But it is really as close as the words we speak, the subjects we study, the dreams we cherish. For if there had been no Greece, we would not be who we are today.

Ideals of Government

Our form of government, democracy, was a Greek invention. The

The philosophy and literature of ancient Greece reach across the ages in Aristotle Contemplating a Bust of Homer, *painted in 1653 by the great Dutch artist Rembrandt.*

government of the United States and other modern democracies is based on the example set by Athens fifteen centuries ago. There are differences, of course. For example, our society is too large for everyone to have a direct voice in all government decisions and acts, so we elect representatives to speak for us. Also, our government, unlike its Athenian model, grants political rights to all social classes, to women, and to foreign-born people who become U.S. citizens. Despite these differences, the basic principles of democracy—government by the governed; trial by jury; freedom of thought, speech, and worship—come to us from the Greeks, untouched by the centuries.

Words and Images

Many of the words we speak every day come from ancient Greece. About one-sixth of the words in the English language are of Greek origin; many of these relate to science and literature. Many English expressions and proverbs, such as *trusting your own eyes*, *second childhood*, and *birds of a feather flock together*, were also common phrases in ancient Greece.

When we put words on paper, we owe another great debt to the Greeks. English grammar, punctuation, and paragraphing all began in ancient Greece. Many of our styles of literature trace their history back to the Greeks, including drama, pantomime (stories acted out without words), history writing, biography, essays, and novels. Oratory—the art of public speaking—also was a Greek invention. And the literature written by the Greeks themselves, especially Homer's epics and the great Golden Age dramas, have inspired modern authors and artists to some of their finest creations.

It is not only the themes of Greek literature and art—those timeless tales of gods and heroes—that have influenced modern artists. Since the

The majesty of ancient Greece's temples has inspired architects down through the centuries—including those who designed the U.S. Supreme Court building in Washington, D.C.

Renaissance, painters and sculptors also have sought to recapture the Greek ideals of perfect beauty and expressiveness. The colorful murals that brighten many public buildings today are descendants of the ancient Greek frescoes.

We see the influence of Greek architecture as well in nearly every European and American city. The grace and strength of Greek temple design stands tall in thousands of modern government buildings, schools, churches, libraries, and museums.

Mind and Spirit

Mathematics, geometry, geography, astronomy, meteorology—the words are Greek, and so are the ideas they stand for. The ancient Greeks laid the foundation for these and many other fields of math and science. In separating science from mythology, the Greeks also invented a brand-new way of thinking about the world. Their love of reason drove them to look for logical answers to nature's mysteries. The same spirit inspires scientific research today.

Like its scientists, ancient Greece's philosophers used logic

The legacy of ancient Greece surrounds us, on city streets and neighborhood porches across America.

to unlock mysteries. But the philosophers' territory was the world within us all. From their wisdom came many ideas that we take for granted. Greek philosophers believed in the worth of the individual. They believed that liberty was more important than blind

Concertgoers take a giant step back in time for a musical performance at the Odeon Theatre, built in 101 C.E. on the slope of the Acropolis in Athens.

SPEAKING GREEK

Here are just a few of the thousands of words that came into English from the ancient Greek language.

**Words for
science and learning**
antiseptic
biology
ecology
geometry
mathematics
philosophy
school

**Words for literature
and the arts**
comedy
drama
episode
grammar
orchestra
poet
tragedy

Words for government
democracy
despot
monarch
politics
tyrant

Everyday words

air	daffodil
anchor	gymnasium
butter	hero
church	squirrel
cube	stadium

THE OLYMPIC GAMES

Much of our modern interest in athletics and physical fitness had its roots in ancient Greece. The Greeks idolized physical beauty, health, strength, and they worked all their lives to stay in top condition. They created gymnasiums for exercise and stadiums for competition. To test and show off their physical skills, they also developed many different kinds of athletic games.

The most famous Greek games were the Olympics. Every four years, beginning in the eighth century B.C.E., the Olympic Games inspired a month-long holiday throughout Greece. All work and wars ceased as thousands journeyed to Olympia to compete and watch the contests. The most important five events, called the pentathlon, combined a footrace, the broad jump, discus throwing, javelin throwing, and wrestling. Other sports included boxing, horseback racing, and chariot racing. A crown of wild olive leaves was the Olympic champion's only prize, but the award brought fame and honor across the land.

The Romans banned the Olympic Games at the end of the fourth century C.E. Then, after fifteen hundred years, the games were revived. The first modern Olympic Games were held in Athens in 1896. Today the games attract amateur athletes from more than one hundred countries to cities all around the globe.

Winning athletes parade triumphantly at the first modern Olympic Games, in Athens, 1896.

obedience and wisdom more important than wealth. They taught that a worthwhile life was one spent in search of understanding, self-improvement, and happiness.

When we accept these ideas as our own, we reach back through time to the ancient Greeks. These curious, creative, adventurous people helped shape our arts and sciences, our ideas and ideals. They are the ancestors of a thousand aspects of our lives. In a way, we all are Greeks.

The Ancient Greeks: A Time Line

Bronze Age

3000 B.C.E.

c. 3000–1200 B.C.E.   c. 1200–800 B.C.E.   c. 800–500 B.C.E.

Bronze Age	Dark Age	Archaic Period

c. 1700–1450
Height of Minoan
civilization

c. 1200–1100
Mycenae
invaded by
unknown forces

776
First known documented
Olympic Games

c. 1400
Height of Mycenaean
civilization

c. 1100–1000
Migrations to Ionia

c. 750–700
Homer writes *Iliad*
and *Odyssey*

c. 1200
Trojan War

c. 900
Migrations to
Aegean islands

c. 750–550
Age of colonizing by
city-states

c. 700
Poet Hesiod catalogs
the gods

c. 610
Use of coined money
begins in Greece

c. 600
Temple of Apollo built
at Delphi

c. 580
Beginnings of Greek
philosophy and
science

507
First democratic
reforms in
Athens

30 B.C.E.

c. 500–400 B.C.E.

Classical Period or Golden Age

c. 500
Temple of Zeus built at Olympia

490–448
Greco-Persian Wars

c. 484
Historian Herodotus born

472
aywright Aeschylus wins first prize in Athenian drama competition

462
Scientist Anaxagoras begins work in Athens

461–429
Pericles leads Athens

c. 460
Historian Thucydides born

447–438
Parthenon built in Athens

431–404
Peloponnesian War

431
ywright Euripedes writes *Medea*

429
wright Sophocles writes *Oedipus*

404
Athens surrenders to Sparta

c. 400–330 B.C.E.

Late Classical Period

399
Trial and death of Socrates

387
Plato founds the Academy in Athens

343–339
Aristotle tutors Alexander of Macedonia

338
Macedonian conquest

336–323
Reign of Alexander the Great

c. 330–30 B.C.E.

Hellenistic Age

323–168
Macedonian kingdom rules Greece and Macedonia

323–30
Ptolemaic kingdom rules Egypt

312–64
Seleucid kingdom rules Asia

c. 287
Scientist Archimedes born

c. 275
Scientist Eratosthenes born

200
First Roman victories in Greece

168
Rome conquers Macedonia

86
Rome conquers Athens

69–30
Reign of Cleopatra, last of Ptolemies

GLOSSARY

agora: the great central marketplace of Athens, where citizens shopped, studied, and gathered to discuss philosophy, science, art, and government

archaeologists: scientists who study ancient tools, artwork, monuments, and other objects to learn about a people from the past

chorus: a company of singers and dancers who explained and commented on the action in Greek plays

demigods: mythological figures who were part human, part divine; demigods were more powerful than humans but less powerful than gods

drama: a form of literature that began in ancient Greece as a religious ceremony and developed into plays written to be performed in theaters

Elysian Fields: a mythological paradise of eternal happiness where the souls of a very few great heroes were permitted to dwell after death

epic poetry: long poems that tell stories about the deeds of heroes from history and legends

fresco: a wall painting on plaster

Hellenistic: relating to Greek history, culture, or art in the period after the rule of Alexander the Great

immortal: never-dying; mortals all die one day but immortal gods live forever

legend: a traditional story involving people and sometimes also gods that may be partly based on historical events

metic: free workingmen of Athens who could not become Athenian citizens because one or both of their parents were born outside Greece

minstrels: wandering poet-musicians who helped preserve a people's history by composing and singing songs about legendary heroes and events of the past

myth: a traditional fictional story, usually involving divine beings, that explains the customs or beliefs of a people

Olympian: relating to the all-powerful gods and goddesses who the Greeks believed lived in a palace on the highest mountain in Greece, Mount Olympus

oracle: a shrine where the Greeks believed a god or goddess spoke, answering their questions and giving advice and predictions about the future; *oracle* also can mean the priests or priestess through whom the god or goddess spoke

patron deity: the god or goddess adopted by a city-state as its own special deity, believed to live in the city's temple and to take a particular interest in the affairs of its people

polis (PAH-les)**:** an ancient Greek city-state

shrine: a building constructed for the worship of a god or goddess, open to the people of all city-states

temple: a building constructed by the people of a city-state as a home for their patron god or goddess

underworld: the land of the dead, which the Greeks called Hades

FOR FURTHER READING

Coolidge, Olivia E. *Greek Myths.* Boston: Houghton Mifflin, 1977.

D'Aulaire, Ingri and Edgar Parin. *D'Aulaires' Book of Greek Myths.* New York: Doubleday, 1962.

Loverance and Wood. *Ancient Greece.* New York: Viking, 1993.

McCaughrean, Geraldine. *Greek Myths.* New York: Macmillan, 1992.

Osborne, Mary Pope. *Favorite Greek Myths.* New York: Scholastic, 1989.

Pearson, Anne. *Eyewitness Books: Ancient Greece.* New York: Alfred A. Knopf, 1992.

Stapleton, Michael. *The Illustrated Dictionary of Greek and Roman Mythology.* New York: Peter Bedrick Books, 1986.

BIBLIOGRAPHY

Asimov, Isaac. *Words from the Myths.* London: Faber and Faber, 1963.

Bowra, C. M., and editors of Time-Life Books. *Great Ages of Man: Classical Greece.* New York: Time-Life Books, 1965.

Bury, J. B. *A History of Greece.* New York: Modern Library, 1913.

Coolidge, Olivia E. *Greek Myths.* Boston: Houghton Mifflin, 1977.

D'Aulaire, Ingri and Edgar Parin. *D'Aulaires' Book of Greek Myths.* New York: Doubleday, 1962.

Durant, Will. *The Life of Greece.* New York: Simon and Schuster, 1966.

Duthie, Alexander. *The Greek Mythology: A Reader's Handbook.* Edinburgh: Oliver and Boyd, 1967.

The Encyclopedia of Classical Mythology. Englewood Cliffs, New Jersey: Prentice-Hall, 1965.

Fine, John V. A. *The Ancient Greeks: A Critical History.* Cambridge, Massachusetts: Harvard University Press, 1983.

Green, Peter. *Ancient Greece: An Illustrated History.* New York: Viking, 1973.

Hale, William Harlan. *The Horizon Book of Ancient Greece.* New York: American Heritage, 1965.

Loverance and Wood. *Ancient Greece.* New York: Viking, 1993.

McCaughrean, Geraldine. *Greek Myths.* New York: Macmillan, 1992.

Osborne, Mary Pope. *Favorite Greek Myths.* New York: Scholastic, 1989.

Payne, Robert. *Ancient Greece: The Triumph of a Culture.* New York: W. W. Norton & Co., 1964.

Pearson, Anne. *Eyewitness Books: Ancient Greece.* New York: Alfred A. Knopf, 1992.

Pope, Maurice. *The Ancient Greeks: How They Lived and Worked.* London: David & Charles, 1976.

Richardson, Donald. *Greek Mythology for Everyone: Legends of the Gods and Heroes.* New York: Avenel, 1989.

Stapleton, Michael. *The Illustrated Dictionary of Greek and Roman Mythology.* New York: Peter Bedrick Books, 1986.

INDEX

ABOUT THE AUTHOR

"One of my favorite books when I was young was a collection of Greek myths with beautiful, dreamlike illustrations. I imagined myself riding on white-winged Pegasus, slamming the lid shut on Pandora's box of evils, and warning the Trojans to keep that big wooden horse outside the gates. It has always seemed a magical thing that stories written so long ago found their way through the ages to a young girl reading by flashlight under the covers at night."

Virginia Schomp is an editor and writer whose books for young readers include *The Bottlenose Dolphin* (Macmillan, Dillon Press, 1994). She lives with her husband, Richard, and their son, Chip, in New York's Catskill Mountains, where they enjoy sharing their backyard with white-tailed deer, black bear, badgers, bats, squirrels, and American bald eagles.